Becoming

Buddha

the story of siddhartha

whitney stewart
& sally rippin

HEIAN

For Venerable Geshe Rinchen Choegyal. W.S.

For my goddaughter, Milani,
and her beautiful parents. S.R.

Published in the United States and Canada by
Stone Bridge Press, P.O. Box 8208, Berkeley CA 94707.
Heian is an imprint of Stone Bridge Press.
First paperback edition published in 2009.

Text copyright © 2005 Whitney Stewart.
Illustrations copyright © 2005 Sally Rippin.
Designed by Georgie Wilson.

Printed in South Korea by Tara TPS through Four Colour Print Group.

2013 2012 2011 2010 2009   10 9 8 7 6 5 4 3 2 1

Publisher's Cataloging-in-Publication Data

Stewart, Whitney, 1959–
    Becoming Buddha; the story of Siddhartha / Whitney Stewart & Sally Rippin; |foreword by Tenzin Gyatso|
    p. ill. cm.
ISBN 978-0-893469-56-6
1. Gautama Buddha—Juvenile literature. 2. Buddhists—India—Biography—Juvenile literature. 3. Buddhism—Juvenile literature. 4. Meditation—Buddhism—Juvenile literature. 5. Buddha. 6. Buddhists. 7. Buddhism. 8. Meditation. I. Rippin, Sally. II. Bstan-'dzin-rgya-mtsho. Dalai Lama XIV, 1935–. III. Title.
BQ892.S74 2005
294.3'63

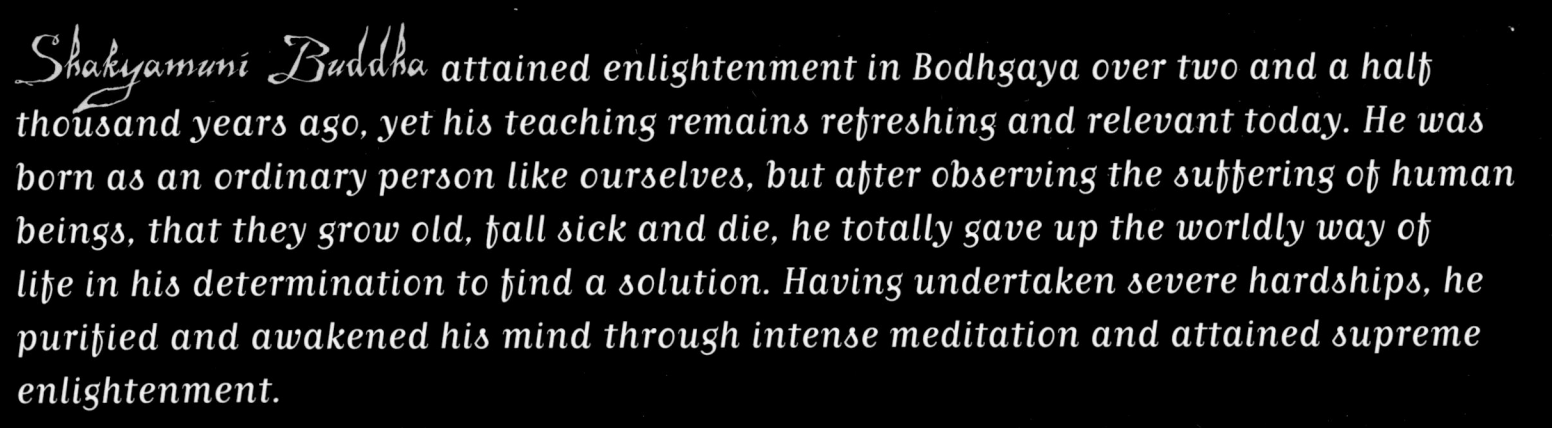

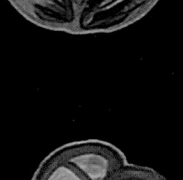

Foreword by Tenzin Gyatso, The 14th Dalai Lama

Shakyamuni Buddha attained enlightenment in Bodhgaya over two and a half thousand years ago, yet his teaching remains refreshing and relevant today. He was born as an ordinary person like ourselves, but after observing the suffering of human beings, that they grow old, fall sick and die, he totally gave up the worldly way of life in his determination to find a solution. Having undertaken severe hardships, he purified and awakened his mind through intense meditation and attained supreme enlightenment.

He showed that purifying the mind is not easy. It takes a lot of time and hard work. But this is also true of any human enterprise. You need tremendous will power and determination right from the start, accepting that there will be many obstacles, and resolving that despite them all you will continue until you have attained your goal.

Moved by a spontaneous concern to help others, the Buddha spent the rest of his life as a homeless monk, sharing his experience with everyone who wished to listen. Both his view of interdependence and his advice not to harm anyone, but to help whoever you can, emphasize the practice of non-violence. This remains one of the most potent forces for good in the world today, for non-violence with compassion is to be of service to our fellow beings.

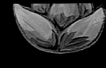

Whitney Stewart's new picture book about the life of the Buddha is timely because even today the story of the Buddha has a lot to tell us. This is not because I have any personal interest in increasing the number of Buddhists in the world, but because I believe that his teaching and his own example can still contribute to global peace and individual happiness. Down the ages the story of the Buddha's life has been retold, giving rise to beautiful carvings and paintings decorating temples and other religious buildings throughout Asia. In telling the story again for contemporary readers, this attractive book is part of that ancient tradition of inspiration.

Tenzin Gyatso
The 14th Dalai Lama

At a time when the oldest bodhi trees in Asia were still in youthful bloom, Queen Maya had a dream. Her sleeping heart told her that a pink lotus blossom was unfolding in her womb. Waking, she saw trees shimmering like amber jewels. The air whispered new songs. Queen Maya was pregnant.

This was a time in India and Nepal when wise men foretold the birth of a child of wisdom, a child to uncover lost truths. When Queen Maya's son was born, she knew he was this gifted child.

Seven days after his birth, Queen Maya died. Her sister became the infant's mother.

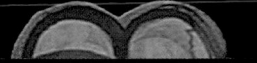

The boy's father, King Shuddhodana, was overjoyed to have a son. He named the boy Siddhartha, 'the one who accomplishes his goal,' and he invited holy men to come and tell the child's future.

The mystic, Asita, entered the palace.

'Truly a great wonder has appeared in the world,' said the weeping Asita, staring into young Siddhartha's eyes.

'My son will be a great king,' Shuddhodana said.

'Your son may become a king,' replied Asita. 'But, should he ever leave the palace, his heart will be torn with sorrow. He will see the hungry, the sick and the dying, and he will want to save them. He will be more than a king; he will be the sun, the moon and the infinite sky of love and compassion.'

'Then why are you crying? Do you foresee misfortune?' the King asked.

'No. I cry because I am old,' replied Asita. 'And I will never hear the teachings of this Buddha.'

And with those words, Asita folded his palms together at his heart and departed.

King Shuddhodana worried about Asita's prediction. 'My son can become a holy man when he is old,' he said to his attendants. 'Until then, he will be a great ruler.'

*I*nside the palace walls, Prince Siddhartha grew up to be a young man of grace and intelligence. His eyes were pools of rich light, and he could see into the hearts of people around him.

But his understanding of the world was small. He knew nothing beyond his easy life of riches and pampering.

Not everyone cherished the young Siddhartha. His half-brother, Devadatta, envied Siddhartha's charm.

*W*hen the two studied side by side, Devadatta shouted out his lessons to drown Siddhartha's voice. When they practiced warrior arts, Devadatta foiled his brother's aim. And when Siddhartha courted his chosen love, Yashodhara, Devadatta tried to steal her. But, Yashodhara preferred Siddhartha's sweet nature and agreed to marry him. Devadatta turned away, defeated by his own meanness and jealousy.

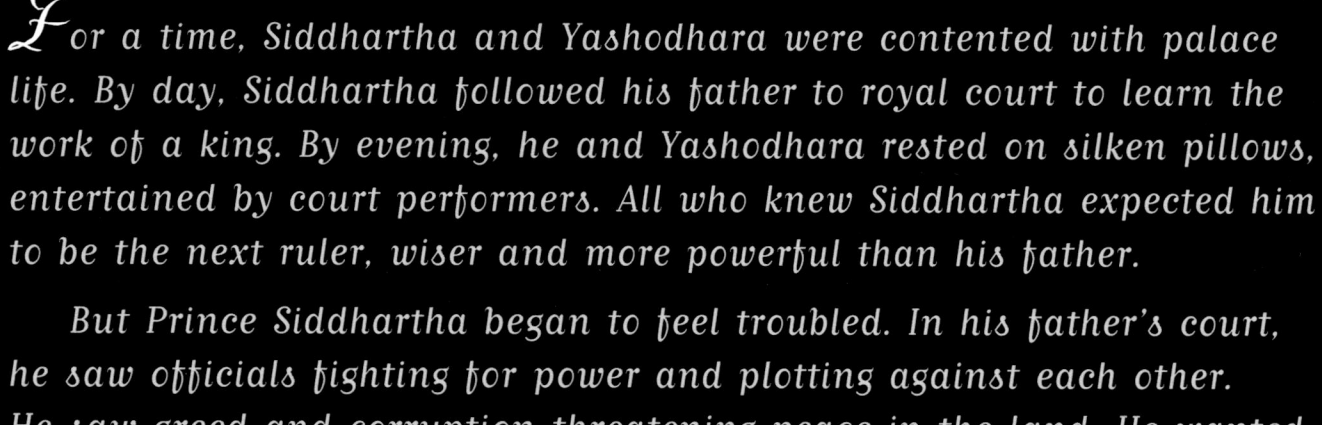

For a time, Siddhartha and Yashodhara were contented with palace life. By day, Siddhartha followed his father to royal court to learn the work of a king. By evening, he and Yashodhara rested on silken pillows, entertained by court performers. All who knew Siddhartha expected him to be the next ruler, wiser and more powerful than his father.

But Prince Siddhartha began to feel troubled. In his father's court, he saw officials fighting for power and plotting against each other. He saw greed and corruption threatening peace in the land. He wanted no part of politics.

Siddhartha wondered if he had another destiny. He decided to see the world outside the palace walls. He asked his charioteer, Chandaka, to drive him through the nearby city of Kapilavastu. Along the way, Siddhartha saw a world he didn't know.

He saw a withered man and did not understand that the man was old. He saw a moaning woman and looked upon a dying person for the first time. He saw a body wrapped in cloth and was confused by the funeral scene before him. These were sights his father had hidden from him. Scenes of pain and misery.

'Is life always so full of suffering?' Siddhartha asked. 'Is there no cure?' His heart felt opened and raw.

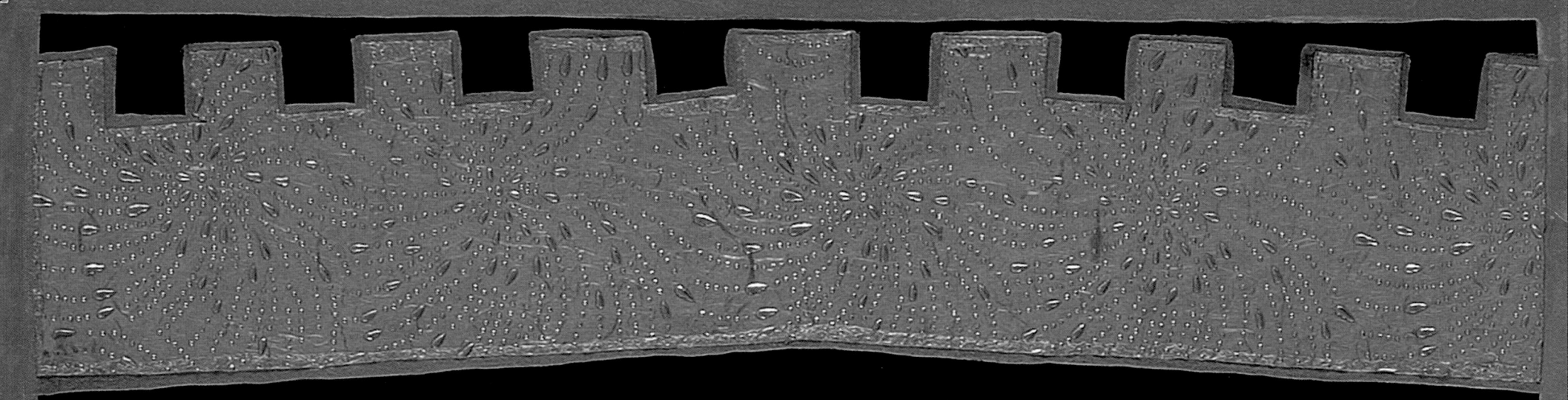

And then Siddhartha spotted a wandering monk. In simple cloth robes, the monk walked slowly, holding out his begging bowl for villagers to fill with food. The monk smiled upon the people as he passed.

'Who is that man in robes, and why does he look so peaceful?' Siddhartha asked Chandaka.

'He is a monk who has given up ordinary life to practice meditation,' Chandaka answered. 'He is looking for peace from life's confusion.'

'That is what I must do,' said Siddhartha.

A
nd so Siddhartha gave up his wealth, his royal title and his family life. Too sad to say goodbye to Yashodhara and their newborn son, Siddhartha fled the palace into a misty night. Dressed now in simple robes, Siddhartha walked through the forest, seeking a teacher of meditation.

After days of wandering, Siddhartha came upon a holy master named Arada and asked if there was more to life than greed, sickness, old age and death. He wanted to know what caused suffering, and what cured it. Arada looked at him with kindness.

'I will teach you to meditate,' said Arada. 'And you will grasp a deeper truth once you have calmed your mind and looked into your heart.'

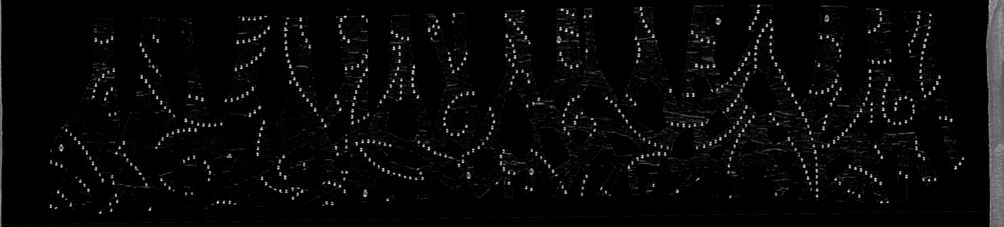

Siddhartha listened to his new teacher, and sat on the forest floor to learn meditation. He tried to concentrate his mind on his breath and let go of his thoughts of Yashodhara's beauty, of his favorite foods back home and of his father's disappointment in him for not becoming a king. If his mind jumped to new thoughts, he learned to pay no attention to them and they faded. Soon Siddhartha could meditate for hours. But still he had not found the cause and cure for suffering. When he was not meditating, his mind still fluttered and jumped.

'I am grateful for your teachings,' Siddhartha told his master. 'But there is still more to understand. I seek full enlightenment and an end to human suffering.'

'I have taught you all I know,' Arada replied.

Siddhartha believed that he still had to conquer his mind and body, and all his moods, desires and fears. Otherwise he would remain caught in suffering. But how could he calm his inner storms? He traveled on, looking for a method.

Deep in the forest, Siddhartha met five men who practiced hardships to conquer their desires, sensations and fears. They ate almost nothing, controlled their breathing and denied themselves sleep. Siddhartha joined these five men and lived with them until he was a rack of bones. He learned to sit in meditation for days, ignoring hunger, sleep, rainstorms, heat and wild animals. But still his mind was not free of suffering.

'I am close to death and have not found enlightenment,' Siddhartha said, looking at his frail body.

And so Siddhartha gave up this harsh method of controlling his desires. His five companions were disgusted by his defeat, and left him alone in the forest. Siddhartha reflected on his life and suddenly remembered a moment from his childhood when he had felt deep calm while sitting in the shade of a large tree. He had experienced a natural state of mind free from the distraction of his senses. Was that a glimpse of enlightenment? he wondered.

'I did not see the truth when I thought of nothing but wealth and beauty,' Siddhartha said to himself. 'And I did not see it when I tortured my body and gave up everything. There must be a middle way.'

Siddhartha then hobbled to a nearby river to bathe. After washing, he sat down in a grove of trees to rest his weakened, starving body. A young village girl, Sujata, saw how hungry Siddhartha looked and brought him a bowl of sweetened rice. He ate, and the rich food gave him strength to travel on.

One day, Siddhartha
met a grass-cutter who offered him tufts
of soft kusha grass, and with it he made himself a
seat at the base of a bodhi tree. He decided to sit there in
silence, in complete relaxation. Facing east, he made a vow.

'I will not move from this seat until I have awakened in full
enlightenment. Even if my life is threatened, I will remain seated here.'

Siddhartha settled into meditation posture and focused his mind on the
quiet between his thoughts. But then his shadow self, Mara, began to speak
to him, to distract him, to clutter his mind.

'Go back to your wife and child,' ordered Mara. 'They miss you.'
Knowing the voice was nothing but his own doubt, Siddhartha did not listen,
and the voice faded.

'You were meant to be a mighty king, not a holy man,' Mara taunted.
Knowing this voice was nothing but his own pride, Siddhartha did not listen,
and it faded into quiet again.

'Who do you think you are, sitting here?' Mara challenged Siddhartha. 'Can
anyone prove you deserve to gain enlightenment?'

With confidence, Siddhartha stretched out his right hand and touched the earth with his fingertips.

'The earth is my witness,' Siddhartha said, and a loud rumbling and shaking came from the ground. 'The earth has seen me struggle on the path to enlightenment.'

And then Mara's voice fell silent.

Siddhartha's mind was steady. No trace of inner darkness blinded him. Free from pride, doubt and fear, from anger, excitement and sorrow, Siddhartha had clear vision. He saw that he was part of an expanse of light that held all beings in the universe. He became a Buddha, an enlightened one, free from all suffering.

But then the Buddha realized that other people needed a path out of suffering, and that he would have to teach them. But how could he explain this light that held everyone? He sat for days under the bodhi tree, his mind resting on this question.

*F*inally the Buddha was ready to teach others what he had learned. He taught them these Four Noble Truths.

Life is a cycle of suffering called samsara, an endless cycle of birth, death and rebirth.

Suffering is caused by desire for pleasure and avoidance of difficulty—by thinking only of yourself.

The end of suffering comes when you are free from desire and selfishness.

To eliminate desire and selfishness, you must act with kindness and compassion for all beings, and with an awareness of your mind and heart.

For the next fifty years, Buddha taught the Four Noble Truths. Realizing that no two people understood him in exactly the same way, he developed many lessons, both simple and profound. He left the world with wise words pointing at the truth. He said,

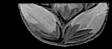

Pay attention to your mind.

Otherwise it will cause you to suffer.

The focused mind brings happiness.

Seeing with compassion, the Buddha understood the heart of anyone
who came to him. Until he was old and wrinkled,
he showed people a way to endless peace.

Siddhartha Gautama is said to have been born in Nepal in about 563 BCE and to have lived until he was in his eighties. When Siddhartha was about thirty-five he reached enlightenment while sitting under a bodhi tree in Bodh Gaya, India. This spot is now a holy shrine for Buddhists. Buddha gave his first teaching in Sarnath, India, another site for Buddhist pilgrimage.

The teachings of the Buddha and his life story were not written down during his lifetime. They were memorized by his followers and recorded hundreds of years later. Because of this, you will find differences in the many versions of Buddha's story.

I have used many sources for this book, including interviews with Buddhist monks and nuns. The details I chose to include were agreed upon by most of my sources. One source stated that although Devadatta was cruel, he did not try to steal away Yashodhara. Other sources claim that Devadatta went so far as to try to murder Siddhartha. For sure, Devadatta never followed his brother's teachings.

After Siddhartha awoke in full enlightenment, he spent about fifty years teaching. His aunt, wife and son all went to him and became his students. Even Siddhartha's father overcame his grief for his departed son and followed the Buddha's wisdom.

Illustrator's Note

When Whitney asked me to illustrate her manuscript I was honored to have the opportunity to work on such an important book, but also very nervous. I am not Buddhist myself, but have a great respect for Buddhism and the Dalai Lama. I knew that in illustrating this book, the challenge for me would be to work with historical images of Siddhartha already created by many wonderful artists over hundreds of years, but also to bring to each picture my own interpretation of Whitney's text.

I began by collecting together as many beautiful materials and images of Siddhartha as I could find to inspire me. From there I began to paint Siddhartha the way that he appeared to me in my mind. While I painted each illustration, I practiced the Dalai Lama's meditation exercises in this book and worked to create the most peaceful and beautiful image I could, all the while aiming to represent the light and compassion that Siddhartha, and now the Dalai Lama, bring to this world.

How to Meditate

A Suggestion from His Holiness the Dalai Lama

Through meditation, the Buddha experienced what some call clear light. There are many ways to meditate. Different teachers use different methods, and the Dalai Lama gave me this method to teach chldren. A simple way to begin is to sit comfortably on the floor or in a chair. Keep your back straight but not strained. Feel relaxed and begin breathing slowly and deeply. You may close your eyes, or keep them open slightly and fixed on a point in front of you. Place your tongue lightly on the roof of your mouth behind your teeth. Keep breathing slowly, but without strain.

Now think of a favorite object or place—perhaps something as simple as a flower or as elaborate as a golden palace. In your mind, draw that object or place as beautifully as you can. Use details. Think of its shape, its design, its color, its texture and its smell. If your mind wanders, bring it back to your design. Keep breathing slowly and deeply. Keep drawing your mental design.

If a distracting thought comes into your mind—such as 'A chocolate ice-cream cone with sprinkles would be good right now'—just notice that thought and bring your mind back to your design. If another thought comes, do the same.

Try to meditate on your design for five minutes. If five minutes is easy, try ten. Try twenty. Stay relaxed, with your mind focused. Experience the calm of meditation.

W.S.

Acknowledgments

The author wishes to thank His Holiness the 14th Dalai Lama,
Tenzin N. Taklha, Tenzin Geyche Tethong, Rakra Tethong,
Geshe Rinchen Choegyal, Lobsang Yeshi, Kalsang Wangmo,
Ngawang Legshe, Susannah Driver-Barstow, Kendra Marcus,
Alison Ribush, Helen Chamberlin, and Sally for their help with this story.

The illustrations in this project have been
assisted by the Commonwealth Government
through the Australia Council, its arts funding
and advisory body.